M'LISS RAE HAWLEY

MARINER'S MEDALLION

Using Foundation Paper Piecing

Martingale
& COMPANY

BOTHELL, WASHINGTON

CREDITS

President . . . . Nancy J. Martin
CEO/Publisher . . . . Daniel J. Martin
Associate Publisher . . . . .Jane Hamada
Editorial Director . . . . Mary V. Green
Design and Production Manager . . . . Cheryl Stevenson
Text and Cover Designer . . . . .Trina Stahl
Technical Editor . . . . .Ursula Reikes
Copy Editor . . . . .Liz McGehee
Illustrator . . . . Laurel Strand
Photographer . . . . Brent Kane

That Patchwork Place, Inc., is an imprint of Martingale & Company.

MISSION STATEMENT
We are dedicated to providing quality products
and service by working together to inspire creativity and
to enrich the lives we touch.

Mariner's Medallion Using Foundation Paper Piecing
© 1999 by M'Liss Rae Hawley

Martingale & Company, PO Box 118, Bothell, WA 98041-0118 USA

Printed in the United States of America
04 03 02 01 00 99   6 5 4 3 2 1

Library of Congress Cataloging-in-Publication Data
Hawley, M'Liss Rae,
Mariner's medallion using foundation paper piecing / M'Liss Rae Hawley.
p.   cm.
ISBN 1-56477-246-2
1. Patchwork—Patterns.   2. Quilting—Patterns.   3. Patchwork quilts.   I. Title.
TT835.H347   1999
746.46'041—dc21   98-30689
                                             CIP

DEDICATION

TO MY HUSBAND, Michael, my rock. Twenty years of encouragement! I can always count on him for an opinion on color, shape, or composition (solicited or not). Though he has a busy and stressful career in law enforcement, Michael continues to find time to iron, fold, stack, and re-stack more fabric than I will remember.

And to Alexander and Adrienne, our children, who began life sitting on my lap at the Bernina, then under the Bernina. Now, they sit next to me and my Bernina, talking, doing their homework, and watching videos. They help me wash and iron fabric, collate pages, and make notebooks for my classes and are a constant source of frustration, inspiration, and joy! I love you all.

ACKNOWLEDGMENTS

I WOULD LIKE to express my sincere gratitude to:

My mother, Josephine W. Frandsen, an executive in the trucking industry long before women traditionally worked outside the home. She always had the time to encourage me emotionally and spiritually. And, yes, she provided me with the financial support to buy more fabric, another loom, yarn, and yet another sewing machine. Her one requirement: that I finish my current project before starting the next one! I love you, Mom!

My father, Kenneth R. Frandsen, by night a Seattle police officer, by day Mr. Mom! My pop provided me the daily necessities, taking me to Singer sewing classes (he fibbed about my age the first year), and always patiently waiting in the parking lot while I picked out more fabric. You are the best!

Though only involved with my life for a mere ten years, Timothy D. O'Connor, M. D., has played a major role in my life. We have weathered many frightening illnesses, and, due largely to his care, I am still a cancer survivor. Thank you, Tim!

Last, but not least, I would like to acknowledge all of my students. They have given me more than I can ever say. I am especially grateful to the quilter friends who so generously entrusted their masterpieces to me and this book. Thank you!

CONTENTS

INTRODUCTION

I LIVE ON AN island. It's the right size: not so large that you forget you are surrounded by water, yet not so small that the sea dominates. My island, Whidbey, sits at the entrance to Puget Sound, a short three miles of salt water from the urban congestion of metropolitan Seattle. By day, the view from my studio deck includes skyscrapers, mountains, and whitecaps. I can also view the many trees we have planted, including lodgepole pines, Douglas firs, and hundreds of filbert trees. Our trees, fields, flowers, and water attract many birds, including one of my favorites, Canada geese.

At night, the rhythmic crisscrossing of lighthouse beams dance across the clouds. In the early-morning stillness, before the fog has lifted, there is no view. None, except those painted in my mind by the groans of distant horns warning mariners of dangerous shoals.

Bernina of America recently featured me and my work in a national ad campaign. Flatteringly, it was entitled "Portrait of the Artist." But what really struck home was the text included in the advertisement. It really did capture my true passion for sewing, quilting, and fabric design. During one of the initial interviews, I blurted out, "I am not sure if I fit sewing into my life, or my life into sewing!" After some reflection, I can truthfully say it is the latter. I cannot visualize myself in a world without fabric, needles, and thread. They are the brushes, paints, and canvases with which I can capture a slice of the world.

The Mariner's Medallion quilt featured in this book begins with the traditional Mariner's Compass. It's the center and therefore the theme of the quilt! Many of the fabrics used in the cover quilt came from another far-off island: Japan. Emi and Kaoru, two Japanese exchange students who stayed with us, brought fabrics to me. These gifts are used throughout the quilt. The chrysanthemum in the center is from an antique kimono. Integrating ethnic materials, old and new, especially fabric that has been given from the heart, makes for the most special of quilts!

I am eternally grateful to Bernina of America and That Patchwork Place, who took a chance on me and The Mariner's Medallion quilt. The Mariner's Medallion may prove to be your compass, as it has for me, to new quilting directions.

ABOUT THE AUTHOR

M'LISS RAE HAWLEY began her lifelong textile adventure at the age of four, embroidering a pillowcase, and hasn't stopped since! She started teaching sewing in high school, and studied Textiles and Clothing at the University of Washington. She continued her studies in weaving, clothing construction, and design in Central Washington University's graduate program.

Among her many accomplishments have been a one-woman quilt show benefiting Seattle's A Contemporary Theater (ACT), second place in Bernina's first annual national professional competition, first place in Washington's Better Homes & Gardens quilt contest (state level), and dozens of local awards. She has been involved in the judging of many local and statewide quilt competitions and has also appeared on local PBS cooking and quilting shows. M'Liss writes haiku as a hobby—some of her poems are sprinkled throughout the book—and lives with her husband, two children, five cats, and four dachshunds.

OVERVIEW OF MEDALLION QUILTS

THE MARINER'S MEDALLION is a framed or medallion-style quilt in which a planned center is surrounded by a series of borders or frames. Medallion quilts may be traced back to the late-eighteenth century, both in America and Europe. They began as large, almost whole-cloth quilts, with sunbursts and large stars as a common center theme, and were often the maker's finest work. Medallion quilts were often considered "best" quilts, used only for company or special occasions.

In the early part of the nineteenth century, panels were manufactured specifically for use in the center of these quilts. These were especially popular in early English patchwork coverlets and quilts, but Americans, particularly wealthy ones, could afford to include them in their own quilts as well.

In the nineteenth century, bedspreads made on Jacquard looms were imported from France. The design of these bedspreads, particularly their medallion centers, played an important role in the development of American medallion quilts. American women also used kerchiefs as center medallions in their quilts. Early examples show spontaneity and less planning, while later quilts were more formal and consistent.

Today medallion quilts are as unique as the quilter! They require a little more planning than a sampler-type quilt, but are well worth the effort. Once you have made a Mariner's Medallion, you will undoubtedly want to make another.

FABRIC SELECTION AND CARE

MY PRIMARY FABRIC choice is 100% cotton. Cotton is soft, easy to work with, and very forgiving. Polyester-cotton blends are more difficult to work with. They have a tendency to ravel, can be slippery, and may be "wimpy" to the hand.

I do use fibers other than cotton. If it comes down to a color choice, the "right" color will usually win over the fiber content. Also, many fabulous synthetics and novelty-type fabrics are available for specific detail work.

I always prewash my fabrics. I launder the fabric just like the finished project will be cared for, usually in the washer and dryer. This ensures colorfastness and removes any residual chemicals or sizing.

There are many tips for keeping your fabric from fraying while laundering. I think I've tried them all! My way of dealing with ragged ends is simple: buy a little extra fabric and trim the frays with a rotary cutter after washing.

Yardage amounts in this book are based on 42"-wide fabric that is no less than 40" wide after preshrinking.

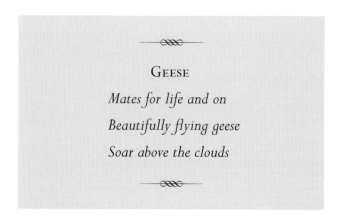

GEESE

Mates for life and on
Beautifully flying geese
Soar above the clouds

SUPPLY LIST

Finished size: 65½" x 81¾"

Materials: 42"-wide fabric

NOTE: *All strips should be cut from the* width *of the fabric, unless otherwise noted.*

Mariner's Compass
- 1¼ yds. background fabric
- ⅓ yd. *each* of 6 different fabrics in varying values (these are your main theme fabrics)

NOTE: *These fabrics may be used elsewhere in the quilt, such as in the Bargello border.*

Flying Geese Border
- ½ yd. background fabric
- ⅜ yd. total of assorted fabrics for geese (use related shades in the same color family)

First Accent Border*
- ¼ yd. contrasting fabric

Plain Border
- ⅜ yd. print fabric

Picket Fence Border
- ¼ yd. background fabric
- ¼ yd. fabric for fence

Twinkle Star Border
- ½ yd. background fabric
- ¼ yd. of 1 fabric or assortment of several fabrics for stars

Sawtooth Stars and Forest Borders
- ½ yd. background fabric
- ⅛ yd. for Sawtooth Stars
- ⅛ yd. *each* of 6 to 10 different fabrics for trees (use the seasonal colors of your trees as a guide: greens, golds, rusts, browns, etc.)
- Assorted brown scraps for tree trunks

Lighthouse and Coast Guard House
Assortment of scraps for:
- Houses (may be same fabric for both)
- Windows (light fabrics or conversation prints, such as faces, flowerpots, or dogs)
- Doors
- Chimney (for Coast Guard House only)
- Roofs
- Header/gutter (for Coast Guard House only)
- Decking (planking, brick, concrete, or other appropriate theme fabric)
- Strips under Lighthouse (pebble and/or rock fabric)

Three Simple Strips
- ⅛ yd. for first strip
- ⅛ yd. for second strip
- ⅛ yd. for third strip

TREES

Leaves float to the ground

Golden, russet, green and brown

Quiet please slow down

Second Accent Border*
- ½ yd. contrasting fabric

Bargello Border
- ¼ yd. *each* of 12 fabrics (high value contrast; can use same fabrics used elsewhere in quilt, such as in the Mariner's Compass)

Last Two Borders
- ½ yd. for narrow border
- 1⅞ yds. for outer border

Binding
- ¾ yd. (may be the same as the final border or a related shade)

Backing
- 4¾ yds.

*If you plan to use the same fabric for the first and second accent borders, purchase a total of ⅝ yard.

Batting
- 72" x 92" piece of batting (twin-size), medium loft

Additional Materials
- Decorative braid or metallic thread for sides and railing on Lighthouse
- Glue or fusible interfacing
- Stitch-n-Tear stabilizer (optional)

LIGHTHOUSE

Guide the Mariner

Lighthouse guide to the harbor

Homeward they are shown

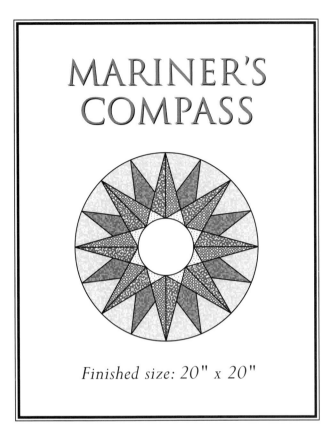

MARINER'S COMPASS

Finished size: 20" x 20"

CUTTING

CUT STRIPS ACROSS the width of the fabric. Label the stacks of strips as you cut them. I recommend that you cut the center circle after the rest of the quilt top is finished (see page 48).

Piece No.	No. of Strips to Cut	Strip Width	Position on Compass
1	2*	2¾"	outer point
2 & 3	4	4¾"	background
4	2	2½"	half of split point
5	2	2½"	half of split point
6	1	3"	inner point

*If you prefer a double point for piece #1, cut 1 strip, 2" wide, from 2 different fabrics: 1 for #1A and 1 for #1B. See step 2 on page 10.

From the background fabric, cut:
- 1 square, 20½" x 20½"

FOUNDATIONS FOR WEDGES

TRACE OR PHOTOCOPY 8 foundations for the wedges (page 13). Cut out the paper foundation on the outside lines. You will need 8 wedges to make the Mariner's Compass, but it doesn't hurt to have a few extras.

STITCHING THE WEDGES

KEEP THE FOLLOWING in mind when paper piecing.

➤ Position the foundation-piecing wedge with the numbers facing you. Always hold the paper the same way, stitching from the center toward the outer edge. This will help you avoid placing the wrong color in the wrong position. Add fabrics to the blank side of the foundation.

➤ Be sure the edge of the strip you are sewing extends at least ¼" beyond the stitching line. Hold the foundation and the fabric strips up to a light source to help you position the strips. You do not want less than ¼". However, if your seam allowance is more than ¼", the strip may not be wide enough to cover the intended space plus the needed seam allowance.

➤ Stitch on the marked side of the foundation, beginning ¼" from the edge of the paper at the center of the compass. Stitch on the line to the opposite edge of the foundation. Backstitch at the edge and stitch ¼" beyond the paper.

➤ Trim seam allowances to ¼" after adding each piece.

➤ Trim the excess strips at least ½" to ¾" beyond the foundation paper after adding each piece. You will trim the excess fabric to an exact ¼" from the edge of the paper later.

➤ Gently press the seam line to help set the stitches in place before opening the pieces.

1. For a single fabric point in piece #1:

a. Place strips #1 and #2, right sides together, on the blank side of the paper under the area marked #1. Be sure the edges extend ¼" beyond the seam line.

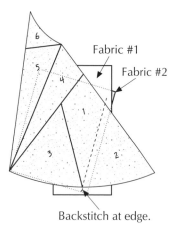

b. Stitch on the line between #1 and #2.

c. Open strip #2 and press toward the area marked #2.

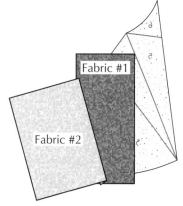

2. For a double fabric point in piece #1:

a. Draw a line from the top point to the bottom point of the area marked #1. This is your new stitching line. Mark the areas #1A and #1B as shown.

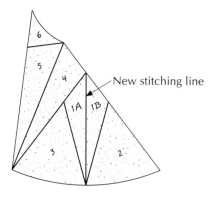

b. Place strips #1A and #1B, right sides together, under the area marked #1A, with a ¼" seam allowance extending beyond the newly drawn stitching line. Stitch on the line between #1A and #1B.

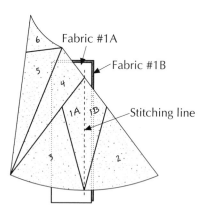

c. Open piece #1B and press toward the area marked #1B. Treat the double-pointed piece as if it were a single point.

d. Place strip #2 on top of piece #1, right sides together, with the edge of strip #2 extending ¼" beyond the seam line. Stitch on the line between #1 and #2. Trim the seam allowances to ¼".

3. Place strip #3 on top of piece #1, right sides together, with the edge of strip #3 extending ¼" beyond the seam line. Stitch on the line between #1 and #3. Trim the seam allowances to ¼". Open strip #3 and press toward the area marked #3.

4. Use strips #4 and #5 to make the split points. Place strip #4 on top of pieces #1/#3. Stitch on the line between #4 and #1/#3. Open strip #4 and press toward the area marked #4.

5. Place strip #5 on top of piece #4. Stitch on the line between pieces #4 and #5. Open strip #5 and press toward the area marked #5.

6. Place strip #6 on top of piece #5. Stitch on the line between pieces #5 and #6. Open strip #6 and press toward the area marked #6.

7. Trim the excess fabrics ¼" from the edge of the paper.

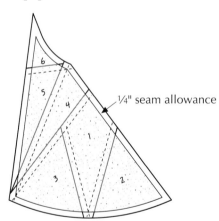

¼" seam allowance

ASSEMBLING THE COMPASS

1. Arrange the 8 wedges in a circle.

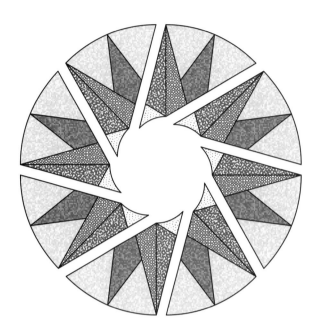

2. With right sides together, join 2 wedges at a time. Be sure to match the seam of pieces #1/#4 with the seam of pieces #5/#6 on the second wedge. Place a pin through the seam intersection, then pin the remainder of the edges together. Sew on the edge of the foundation paper.

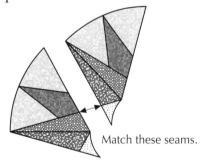

Match these seams.

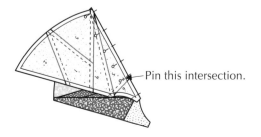

Pin this intersection.

3. Continue sewing the remaining wedges together in the same manner. Join the pairs to complete the circle. Gently press the joining seams in one direction. If your compass is not perfectly flat, adjust the seam allowances accordingly.

4. Using a basting stitch, machine stitch around the outer edge of the Mariner's Compass, along the edge of the paper. This stitching stabilizes the compass and becomes the seam guide for appliquéing the compass to the background fabric.

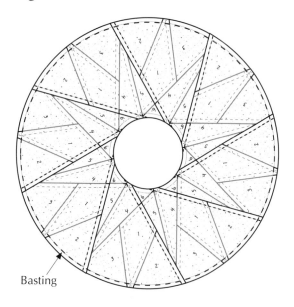

Basting

5. Carefully press along the basting line to the wrong side of the compass. This is your ¼" seam allowance.

6. Carefully remove the paper from the back of the compass. One easy method is to spray the paper with a fine mist of water. Use a seam ripper to gently nudge the damp paper away from the seam.

7. Press the background square (you may wish to starch it while pressing). To find the center of the background square, fold it in half twice and finger-press the center, moving gradually outward. Use the fold lines and the center

point to center the pieced compass on the square. Make certain that the horizontal and vertical lines are "true." Lines that are not true will be an obvious distraction!

8. Pin around the outside edge of the compass. Try not to distort or shift the circle while pinning. Starting from the center of the circle, hand baste with a contrasting-color thread in concentric circles out to the edge of the circle. The basting lines should be about 1" to 2" apart. Remove pins as you go. Be careful not to distort the circle while basting.

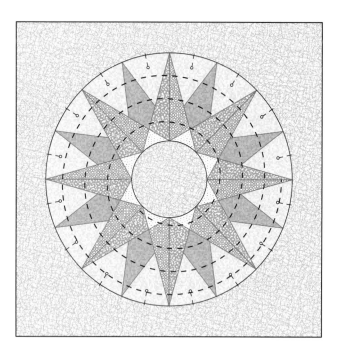

9. Appliqué the compass to the background by hand. Use a thread that matches the background of the Mariner's Compass. If the basting stitches around the perimeter of the compass are visible, carefully remove them with a seam ripper. Do not remove the spiral rows of basting; they will be removed later.

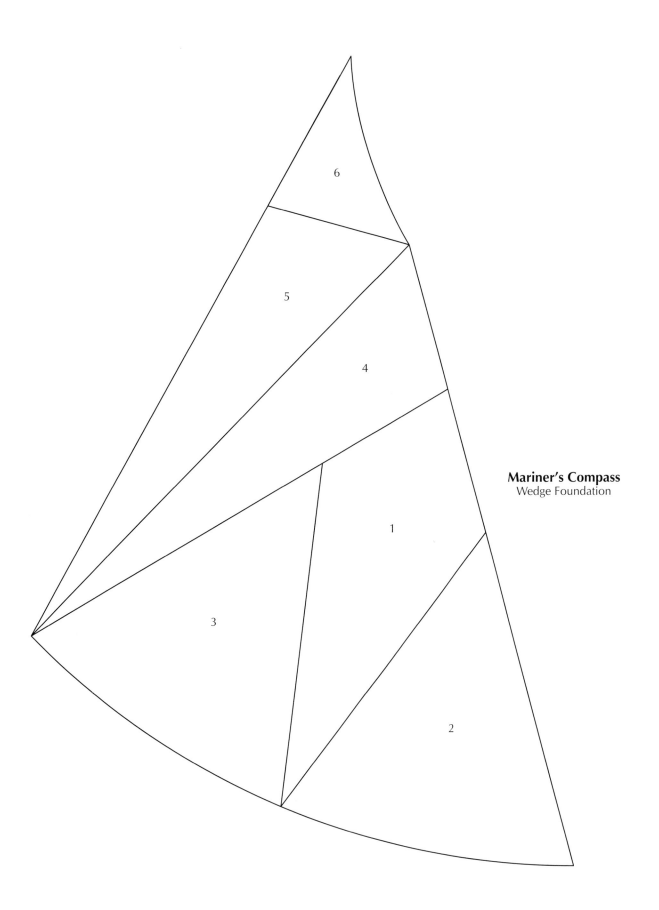

Mariner's Compass
Wedge Foundation

FLYING GEESE BORDER

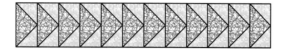

Finished size of unit: 2" x 4"
Finished size of border: 4" x 24"

THE FLYING GEESE border is the first border to surround the Mariner's Compass. The background for the geese may be the same as the background square of the compass since these backgrounds touch. There are many techniques for making these units. This particular method produces four flying-geese units at a time. You will need 48 flying-geese units to fit around the Mariner's Compass.

CUTTING

From the background fabric, cut:
• 48 squares, each 3" x 3". If using the same background fabric for all the geese, cut 4 strips, each 3" wide, then cut the strips into squares.

From the fabric for the geese, cut:
• 12 squares, each 5½" x 5½". If using the same fabric for all the geese, cut 2 strips, each 5½" wide, then cut the strips into squares.

PIECING THE FLYING GEESE UNITS

1. Draw a diagonal line from corner to corner on the wrong side of the 3" background squares.

2. With right sides together, place 2 background squares diagonally on top of a 5½" geese-fabric square. Trim the points where the squares overlap at the center.

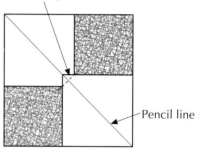

Trim these points.

Pencil line

3. Sew the background squares to the large square, corner to corner, stitching ¼" on each side of the drawn line.

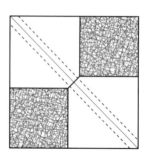

TIP: *A ¼" foot is helpful for this step. You may also be able to move your needle to an appropriate position. If you do not have a ¼" foot or your needle is not adjustable, draw the seam lines with a sharp pencil. Use a drafting ruler for a more accurate line.*

4. Iron or finger-press each side of the background squares toward the middle of the square, and pin them out of the way.

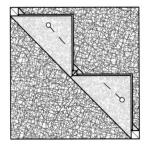

5. Repeat steps 2 and 3 with two more background squares in the remaining corners.

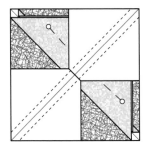

6. Cut on the second diagonal pencil line. Remove the pins, unroll the fabric, and cut on the first diagonal pencil line. Gently press the background fabric away from the geese fabric. Violà—four geese!

7. Repeat steps 2–6 to make a total of 48 flying-geese units.

ASSEMBLING AND ATTACHING THE FLYING GEESE BORDER

1. Join the flying-geese units into 4 border sections, with 12 units in each border. Watch your "goose points"; you don't want to lose these. Press the seams away from the goose points.

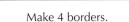

Make 4 borders.

2. Starting in the upper left corner, with your geese pointing toward the right, attach the first Flying Geese border strip to the top of the square. End your stitching 2" from the upper right corner; backstitch. Two flying-geese units will extend beyond the square. Watch for the goose points around the edge of the borders; you may want to pin the points to keep them accurate.

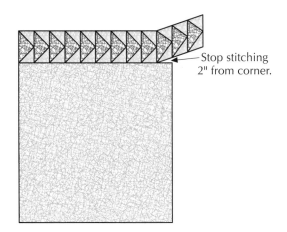

Stop stitching 2" from corner.

3. Attach the remaining Flying Geese borders around the square in the order shown. Complete the partial seam in the upper right corner. Press all the seams toward the center square.

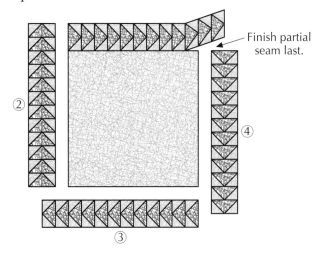

Finish partial seam last.

FIRST ACCENT AND PLAIN BORDERS

THE SECOND BORDER on your medallion is an accent border, the first of two similar accent borders. Although this border is not pieced, it is no less significant. It does just what its name implies; it accents the pieced borders. If you are having trouble deciding on the perfect fabric, a color that is complementary to your Flying Geese border would be a natural. For example, if your geese are red, the complementary accent border would be green as shown in "The Compass to Color" on page 18.

The third border is an unpieced plain border. This border looks best if it is a background fabric. Though it may be different from the previously used backgrounds, it can be the same. Choose a fabric that you like and that will stand on its own.

CUTTING

From the fabric for the first accent border, cut:
- 4 strips, each 1½" x 42"

From the fabric for the plain border, cut:
- 4 strips, each 3" x 42"

ADDING THE BORDERS

1. Measure the quilt through the center horizontally. Trim 2 of the 1½"-wide border strips to this measurement and add them to the top and bottom of the quilt top.

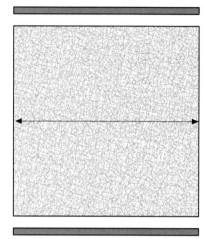

2. Measure the quilt through the center vertically, including the borders you just added. Trim the remaining 1½"-wide border strips to this measurement. Add these to the side edges of the quilt top. Press the seams toward the accent border.

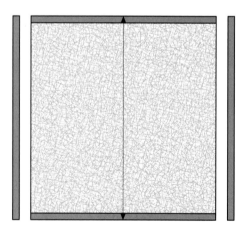

3. Repeat steps 1 and 2 to add the plain (3"-wide) border. Press the seams toward the plain border.

NOTE: *At this point, your quilt top should measure 35½" x 35½", including seam allowances.*

THE GARDEN COURT COMPASS

By M'Liss Rae Hawley, 1997, Freeland, Washington, 63" x 78". M'Liss's island farm was the original inspiration for this quilt. Her husband and father have planted hundreds of trees, while she grows many flowers.

THE COMPASS TO COLOR

By M'Liss Rae Hawley, 1998, Freeland, Washington, 63" x 78". The sections of this quilt started out as M'Liss's class samples. They were so much fun, she decided they had to come out of the notebook and become a quilt.

SUMMER'S MEDALLION

By Gerry Baldeschwiler, 1998, Seattle, Washington, 60" x 74". Quilted by Gerry and Doris Ellis. Gerry's version
of the Mariner's Medallion includes a particularly nice interpretation of the Lighthouse
and Coast Guard House blocks.

LOOKING WEST

By Vicki DeGraaf, 1998, Langley, Washington, 50" x 50". Misty mountains line the right side of Vicki's Mariner's Compass. She oversized her Twinkling Star blocks and shaded them from dark to light, then shaded them back again! Notice the radiating lighthouse in the bottom left corner. This quilt is a masterpiece of contrast and color.

Close-up of *Looking West*

NATURE'S COMPASS

By Karen Mull Griffin, 1998, Seattle, Washington, 70" x 62". Quilted by M'Liss Rae Hawley. Brilliant reds and indigos really make this quilt sing with color. Karen substituted an original-design garden gate and beehive in this version of the Mariner's Compass.

Close-up of *Nature's Compass*

COMPASS IN THE CABIN

By Pat French, 1996, Issaquah, Washington, 76" x 76". Log Cabin blocks form an effective outer border for Pat's rendition of the Mariner's Compass. Note her consistent use of the same background fabric for most of the quilt—all except, that is, for the spunky little house border!

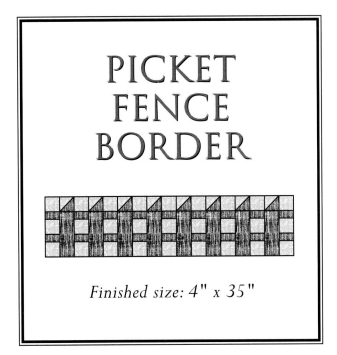

PICKET FENCE BORDER

Finished size: 4" x 35"

YOU CAN USE the same background fabric for the Picket Fence border that you used for the Flying Geese border or the Mariner's Compass block, or you can use the same fabric that you used for the third border, as I did in the quilt on the cover. If you are using several similar backgrounds, just choose one to make the background for the "fence." If your quilt has a theme that lends itself to a perfect fabric, use that one! Just remember to keep your quilt in the same "time zone"; if your geese are flying at night, your fence should also be silhouetted against a dark background.

The Picket Fence border will go across the bottom of the quilt, so you need to decide which side is the bottom.

CUTTING

From the background fabric, cut:
- 9 squares, each $1\frac{7}{8}$" x $1\frac{7}{8}$". Cut squares once diagonally to make a total of 18 half-square triangles for the fence-post points. You will use 17.
- 3 strips, each $1\frac{1}{2}$" x 42", for strips between the fence rails.

From the fabric for the fence, cut:
- 9 squares, each $1\frac{7}{8}$" x $1\frac{7}{8}$". Cut squares once diagonally to make a total of 18 half-square triangles for the fence-post points. You will use 17.
- 2 strips, each $1\frac{1}{2}$" x 42". Cut strips into a total of 17 rectangles, each $1\frac{1}{2}$" x $3\frac{1}{2}$", for fence posts.
- 2 strips, each 1" x 42", for the fence rails.

PIECING THE BORDER

1. Sew a background triangle and a fence triangle together to make a half-square triangle unit. Press the seams toward the fence fabric.

Make 17.

2. Sew the background and fence strips together to make a strip unit. Press the seams toward the background fabric. Cut 18 segments, each $1\frac{1}{2}$" wide, from the strip unit. While cutting, check your measurements and square up the unit whenever needed before cutting more segments.

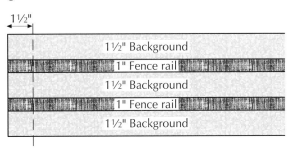

3. Sew the half-square triangle units to the fence rectangles. Be sure the fence triangle is oriented correctly before stitching. Press the seam toward the rectangle.

Make 17.

4. Arrange the units for the fence border, alternating rails and posts. Begin and end with a rail. Join the units and press the seams in one direction.

5. Square up the fence border if necessary. Sew the top of the fence border to the bottom of the third border. Press the seam toward the third border.

PROBLEMS WITH FITTING

IF, FOR SOME reason, the Picket Fence border is too short, add another post or rail segment to one end. If it is too long, remove a rail or a post segment. Your picket fence does not have to begin and end with the same segment. You could also attach the border and trim the outer rails to fit. The end rail segments can be wider or narrower than the other rail segments without being a distraction.

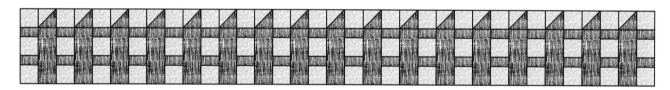

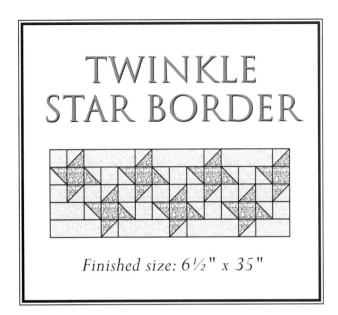

TWINKLE STAR BORDER

Finished size: 6½" x 35"

ONE OR MORE fabrics may be used for the background of this border, although I prefer one interesting background. Many of the star fabrics currently available would work well as the background. The stars come in many colors, shapes, and sizes. If you want to use a light-colored background, try white, beige, or yellow backgrounds with dark stars, such as navy blue, black, or purple. If your quilt has a night theme, use a dark background with light-colored stars. This border will take some time, so make your effort count!

CUTTING

From the background fabric, cut:
- 2 strips, each 1¼" x 42"
- 33 squares, each 1½" x 1½"
- 32 squares, each 1⅞" x 1⅞". Cut squares once diagonally to make a total of 64 half-square triangles.
- 2 rectangles, each 1½" x 2½"
- 16 rectangles, each 1½" x 3½"
- 2 rectangles, each 1½" x 7"

From the fabrics for the stars, cut:
- 16 squares, each 1½" x 1½"
- 32 squares, each 1⅞" x 1⅞". Cut squares once diagonally to make a total of 64 half-square triangles.

PIECING THE BORDER

1. Sew a background triangle and a star triangle together to make a half-square triangle unit. Press the seams toward the star fabric.

Make 64.

2. Arrange and join the half-square triangle units, 1½" squares, and 1½" x 2½" and 1½" x 3½" rectangles in horizontal rows as shown below. Press the seams in opposite directions from row to row.

3. Join the rows. Press the seams toward the bottom of the border.

4. Measure the length of your Twinkle Star border and trim the 1¼"-wide background strips to this length. Add these strips to the top and bottom edges. Press the seams toward the background strips.

5. Sew a 1½" x 7" background rectangle to each end of the border. Press the seams toward the background rectangles. Square up the border if necessary.

6. Attach the Twinkle Star border to the top of the quilt, above the third border.

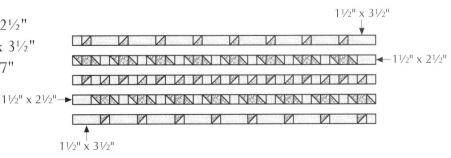

1½" x 3½"

1½" x 2½"

1½" x 2½"

1½" x 3½"

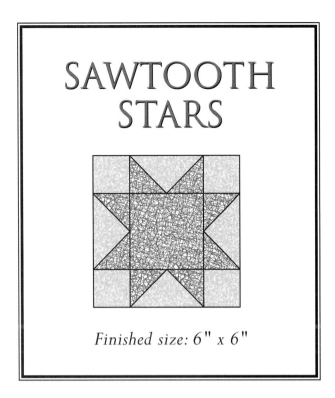

SAWTOOTH STARS

Finished size: 6" x 6"

THE SAWTOOTH STARS are the corner squares between the Twinkle Star border and the Forest borders. Use the same or a similar background fabric for the Sawtooth Stars as you used for the adjacent borders.

CUTTING FOR 2 STARS

From the background fabric, cut:
- 8 squares, each 2" x 2"
- 8 rectangles, each 2" x 3½"

From the fabric for the stars, cut:
- 2 squares, each 3½" x 3½"
- 16 squares, each 2" x 2"

PIECING THE STARS

1. Draw a diagonal line on the wrong side of the 2" star squares. Place a 2" star square on one end of a 2" x 3½" background rectangle, right sides together. Stitch on the diagonal line, from the center of the rectangle to the corner.

Trim the bottom half of the star fabric ¼" from the stitching line. Press the right side of the star fabric over the background fabric.

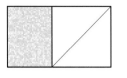 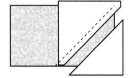

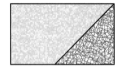

2. Place another 2" star square on the other end of the rectangle. Stitch on the line; trim the seam of the star fabric to ¼" and press. You have just made a double half-square triangle unit.

 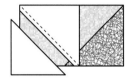

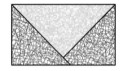

Make 8.

3. Arrange the star units and background squares as shown. Sew the units into horizontal rows, then join the rows.

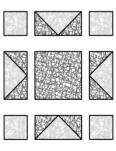

Make 2.

NOTE: *Set the Sawtooth Stars aside for now. They will be sewn to the top of the Forest border later.*

Finished size: 6" x 45½"

MAKING THE STRIP UNIT

1. From a variety of fabrics, cut strips in widths varying from 1" to 2½" wide and 22" long. Use 6 to 10 different fabrics in this unit; the greater the variety, the more interest it creates. Vary the color values for a more natural look.

2. Sew the strips together with ¼"-wide seams. Press the seams in one direction. The strip unit should measure approximately 20" x 22".

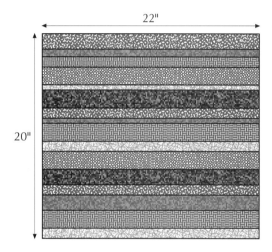

MAKING PLASTIC TEMPLATES

1. Lay the plastic template material over the pattern. Trace the lines of the pattern with a permanent pen.

2. Cut out the shapes with a rotary cutter (used blade) or scissors (not fabric scissors).

3. Label each template with the name of the pattern and the corresponding letter.

TIP: *Store the templates in a plastic zippered bag. Include a 3" x 5" card with the pattern name, size of the block, number of pieces, and the quilt it was used in.*

ALL THE FOREST border trees are cut from a strip unit composed of multiple fabrics. For a spring, summer, or evergreen theme, use a variety of green fabrics. Add embroidered pink French knots to make the filbert trees into blossoming cherry trees. For a fall look, use autumn colors like gold, rust, orange, and brown for your strip unit. Or, add red buttons to the green filbert trees to make them into fall apple trees. For a snowy, wintry look, try white and light gray fabrics. The number and type of trees you make is up to you.

EVERGREEN TREES

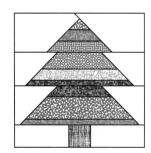

Finished size: 6" x 6"

CUTTING FOR 1 EVERGREEN TREE

From the pieced strip unit, cut:
- 1 of Template A
- 1 of Template C
- 1 of Template E

From the background fabric, cut:
- 2 rectangles, each 1½" x 3"
- 1 each of Template B and B reversed
- 1 each of Template D and D reversed
- 1 each of Template F and F reversed

From the fabric for the trunk, cut:
- 1 square, 1½" x 1½"

PIECING THE TREE

ARRANGE THE PIECES as shown. Sew them together in horizontal rows. Press the seams toward the background fabric. Join the rows.

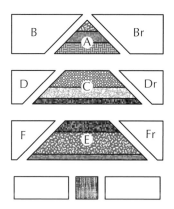

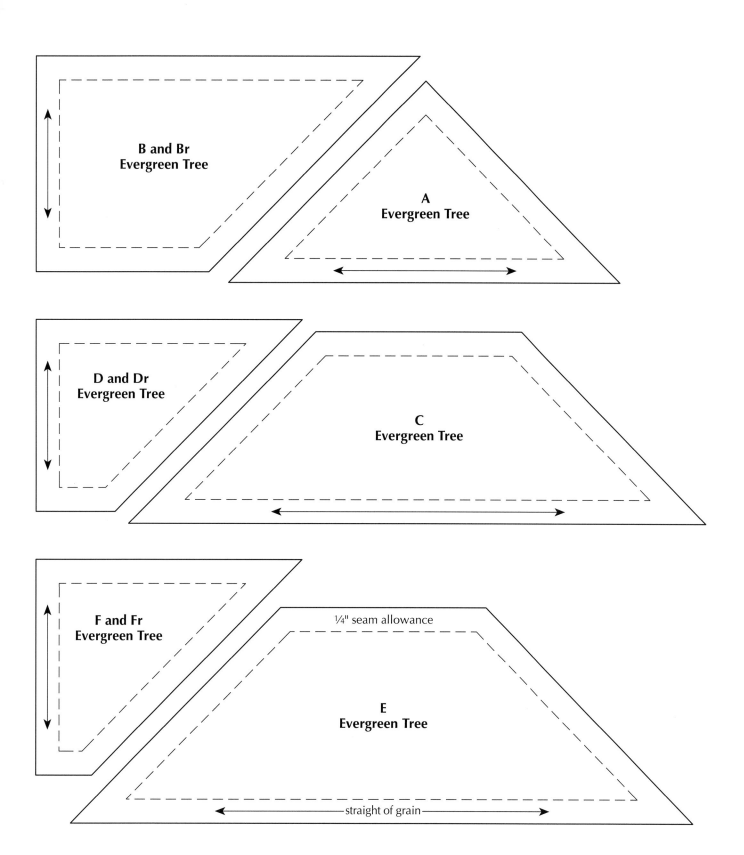

B and Br
Evergreen Tree

A
Evergreen Tree

D and Dr
Evergreen Tree

C
Evergreen Tree

F and Fr
Evergreen Tree

¼" seam allowance

E
Evergreen Tree

straight of grain

DOUGLAS FIR TREE

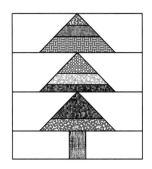

Finished size: 6" x 6½"

CUTTING FOR 1 DOUGLAS FIR TREE

From the pieced strip unit, cut:
- 3 of Template A

From the background fabric, cut:
- 2 rectangles, each 1¾" x 3⅛"
- 3 each of Template B and B reversed

From the fabric for the trunk, cut:
- 1 piece, 1¼" x 1¾"

PIECING THE TREE

ARRANGE THE PIECES as shown. Sew them together in horizontal rows. Press the seams toward the background fabric. Join the rows.

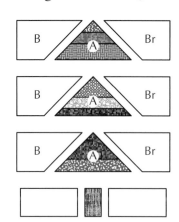

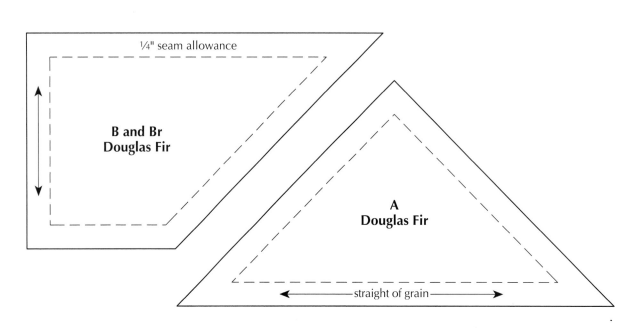

FILBERT TREE

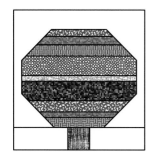

Finished size: 6" x 6¼"

CUTTING FOR 1 FILBERT TREE

From freezer paper, cut:
- 1 Filbert Tree pattern. Lay a piece of freezer paper over the pattern (page 34) and trace the tree. Do not add seam allowances.

From the background fabric, cut:
- 1 rectangle, 5½" x 6½"
- 2 rectangles, each 1¾" x 3"

From the fabric for the trunk, cut:
- 1 rectangle, 1½" x 1¾"

Optional:
- Cut 1 rectangle, 6" x 7", from fabric stabilizer.

MAKING THE TREE

1. Lay the freezer-paper pattern, coated side down, on the wrong side of the pieced strip unit. Press with a dry iron. Cut out the tree, adding a ¼"-wide seam allowance all around. This is easy to do with a rotary cutter, using a ruler to measure the ¼" as you go. Do not remove the freezer paper yet.

2. Using the paper pattern as a guide, press under the ¼" seam allowance around the sides and top of the tree. Do not press the bottom edge under. Carefully fold in the seam allowance at each corner. Remove the freezer paper from the back of the fabric. Press again from the right side.

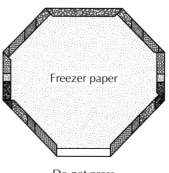

Do not press
bottom edge under.

TIP: *A little spray starch helps at this point.*

3. Position the Filbert Tree on the background fabric, matching the unpressed edge of the tree with the bottom of the 5½" x 6½" background rectangle. Place the piece of fabric stabilizer (if using) on the wrong side of the background rectangle. Pin the tree in place, placing the pins outward. Topstitch the tree in place by machine, using thread to match the tree.

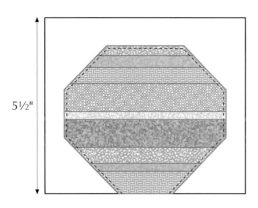

4. Sew a 1¾" x 3" background rectangle on each side of the trunk rectangle. Sew the trunk unit to the bottom of the tree. Press the seam toward the trunk.

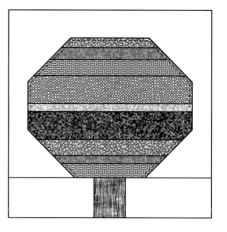

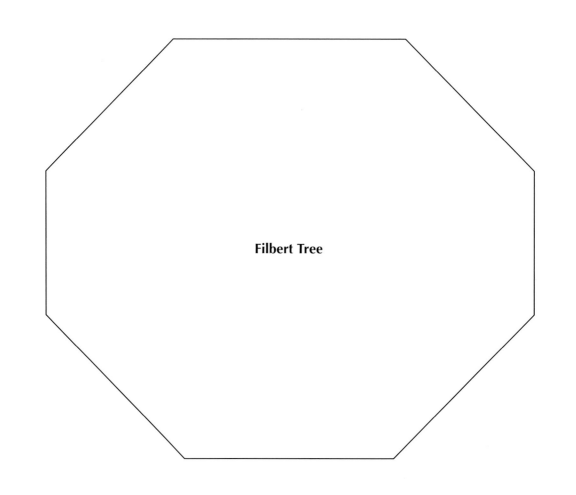

Filbert Tree

LODGEPOLE PINE TREES

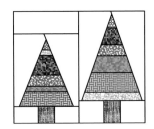

Finished size: 6" x 5"
(2 large trees or 1 small and 1 large)

6" x 4" (2 small trees)

THERE ARE TWO sizes of Lodgepole Pine trees, 3" x 4" and 3" x 5", that can be combined to make a block. You can use two small trees, two large trees, or a small and a large tree. Trace or photocopy the number of foundations you desire. Cut on the outside line of the rectangle.

CUTTING FOR 1 SMALL TREE

From the pieced strip unit, cut:
- 1 square, 3½" x 4" (piece #1)

From the background fabric, cut:
- 2 rectangles, 2½" x 4" (pieces #2 and #3)
- 2 rectangles, each 1¼" x 1⅝"

From the fabric for the trunk, cut:
- 1 square, 1¼" x 1¼"

CUTTING FOR 1 LARGE TREE

From the pieced strip unit, cut:
- 1 rectangle, 3½" x 5" (piece #1)

From the background fabric, cut:
- 2 rectangles, 2½" x 5" (pieces #2 and #3)
- 2 rectangles, each 1½" x 1⅝"

From the fabric for the trunk, cut:
- 1 rectangle, 1¼" x 1½"

PIECING THE TREES

REFER TO THE paper-piecing guidelines on page 9.

1. Place piece #1, right side down, on the blank side of the foundation, under the area marked #1.

2. Place piece #2 on top of piece #1, right sides together. Remember to extend the edge of the pieces ¼" beyond the stitching line. Starting at the top of the tree, stitch on the line between #1 and #2.

3. Press the seam to set the stitches. Trim the seam allowance to ¼". Open piece #2 and press toward the area marked #2.

4. Repeat steps 2 and 3 with piece #3.

5. Trim the excess fabric ¼" from the outside edge of the paper. Remove the paper.

6. Sew a 1⅝"-long background rectangle to each side of the trunk. Press the seams toward the trunk. Join the trunk unit to the tree.

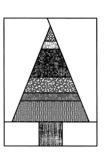 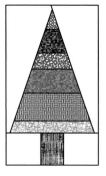

Small Tree   Large Tree

7. Combine small and large trees as desired. If you join a small tree and a large tree, cut 1 rectangle, 1½" x 3", from background fabric. Sew this to the top of the small tree before joining it to the large tree.

Cut filler piece
1½" x 3".

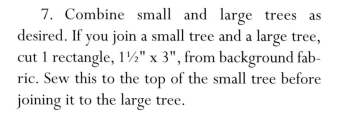

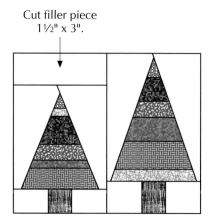

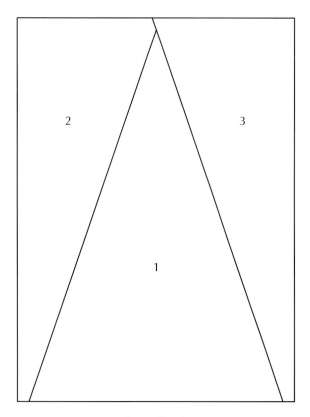

Lodgepole Pines
Large Tree Foundation

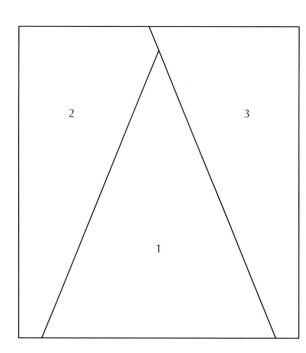

Lodgepole Pines
Small Tree Foundation

Finished size: 6" x 12¼"

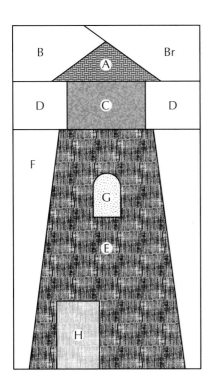

CUTTING

DON'T FORGET TO add ¼"-wide seam allow-lowances all around when cutting appliqué pieces.

From the fabric for the top of the lighthouse, cut:
- 1 of Template A

From the fabric for the light, cut:
- 1 rectangle, 2" x 3", for piece C

From the fabric for the bottom of the lighthouse, cut:
- 1 of Template E

From the background fabric, cut:
- 1 each of Template B and Br
- 2 rectangles, each 2" x 2¼", for piece D
- 1 rectangle, 6½" x 8", for piece F

From additional fabrics for area under the lighthouse, cut:
- 2 different strips, 1¼" x 6½"

Optional:
- Cut 1 of Template G for the window.
- Cut 1 rectangle, 1⅞" x 2⅝", for the door (H).

PIECING
THE LIGHTHOUSE

1. Arrange pieces A, B, Br, C, and D as shown. Sew the pieces together in horizontal rows. Press the seams toward the background. Join the rows.

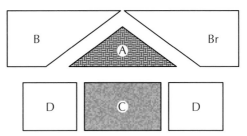

2. Center and appliqué piece E on top of piece F. Appliqué optional pieces G and H now.

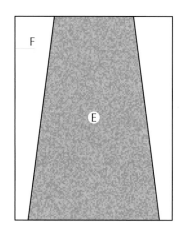

3. Add any vertical embellishments to the lighthouse at this time. See the quilts on pages 17–20 for options. If you are using decorative braid, sew it in place. The ends of the braid will be caught in the seams.

4. Join the roof/light unit to the lighthouse body. Press the seam toward the lighthouse body.

5. Add the 1¼" x 6½" strips to the bottom of the lighthouse. Press the seams toward the bottom of the block. If you want to use just one fabric for this strip, cut 1 strip, 2" x 6½".

EMBELLISHMENT IDEAS

BELOW ARE JUST a few suggestions for adding additional embellishments. I am sure you can add to this list, making your Lighthouse block more personal and interesting.

➤ Add a circle at the top of lighthouse (on piece A). Cut out a small circle, about ½" in diameter. Attach with glue or fusible interfacing.

➤ Add a circular window in the center of the lighthouse, about a quarter of the way down from the top light.

➤ Try two windows instead of one.

➤ If your lighthouse has a door, add a doorknob. I have used a button, but a bead would also work. If you can't find the right color of button, a few layers of fingernail polish on a plastic button will change its color.

➤ A railing around the base of the light adds an important touch. You can use metallic thread to stitch the railing by machine. Or, you can attach gold or brass-colored trim to make the railing.

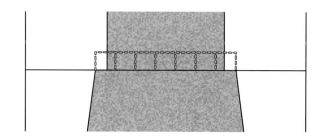

Here's how to machine stitch the railing:

1. Use a pencil to lightly draw the railing onto the lighthouse.

2. Place a piece of fabric stabilizer (Stitch-n-Tear) under the railing area. Set your machine to a satin stitch. Attach an appliqué foot if your machine has one. Use metallic thread and a machine needle designed for the thread.

3. Practice on a scrap of fabric first. When you have the stitch length and width desired, stitch the railing, following the pencil lines.

Here's how to attach a gold or brass trim for the railing:

1. Use a pencil to lightly draw the railing onto the lighthouse.

2. Lay the trim on the pencil lines and cut it accordingly.

3. Hand stitch or glue the trim in place.

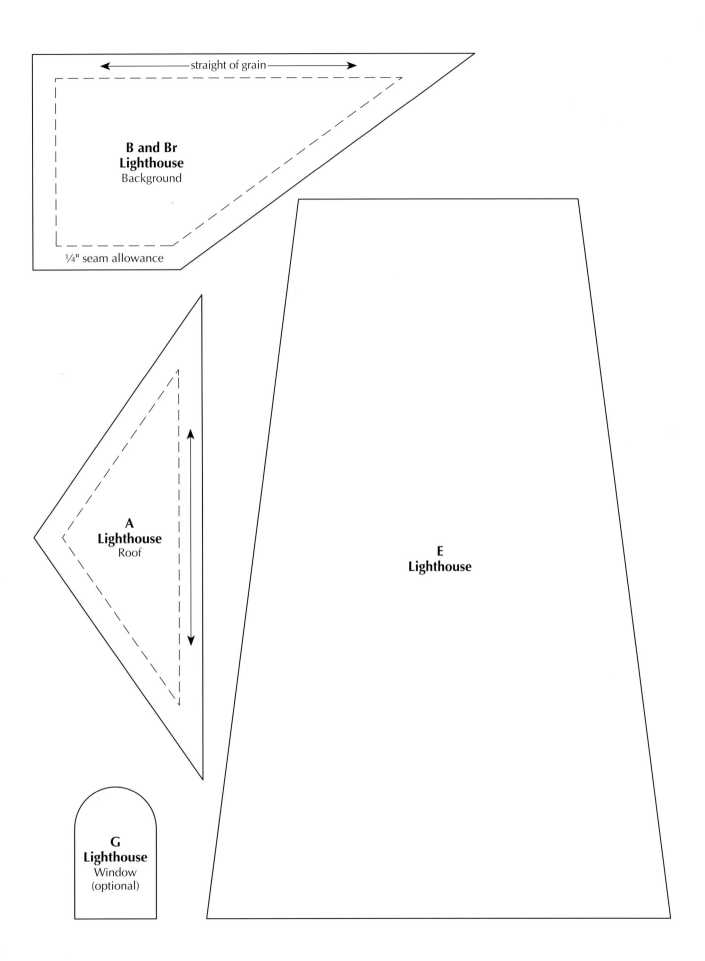

straight of grain

B and Br
Lighthouse
Background

¼" seam allowance

A
Lighthouse
Roof

E
Lighthouse

G
Lighthouse
Window
(optional)

COAST GUARD HOUSE

Finished size: 6" x 9¾"

Another option would be to make twice as many half-square triangle units as needed. You will end up with two that work and two that do not. Put the two unworkable units in a bag; label them with their cut and finished dimensions. You may use them someday.

CUTTING

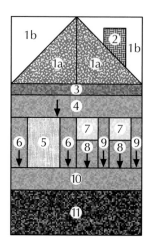

IF YOU USE directional prints for your house, such as a stripe or a one-way design, you must take extra care when cutting the pieces so that the fabric runs in the same direction. For example, if you use a directional print for the siding, you must cut all the house pieces with the fabric running in the same direction (see arrows in illustration at right).

The directions for making this block assume you will be sewing two half-square triangles together to make the units required for the roof and background. There is a potential problem, however. If one or both of the fabrics for the roof and background are directional, the fabric in one unit will face the proper direction and the other unit will look wrong.

One way to deal with this is just to use it as is. Another way is to make templates for the roof and background instead of making half-square triangle units. You will need one roof and a background triangle and its reverse.

Cut the following pieces from assorted fabrics.

Piece No.	No. of Pieces to Cut	Dimensions
1a (roof)	1	3⅞" x 3⅞", cut once diagonally
1b (background)	1	3⅞" x 3⅞", cut once diagonally
2 (chimney)	2	1½" x 2½"
3 (header)	1	1" x 6½" (not the same color as house)
5 (door)	1	2" x 2¾"
7 (windows)	2	1½" x 1½" (Use a light-colored fabric or a theme fabric, for example, a dachshund in the window.)

Cut the following pieces for the house from the same fabric; remember to pay attention to the direction of the print if you are using a directional fabric.

Piece No.	No. of Pieces to Cut	Dimensions
4	1	1½" x 6½"
6	2	1¼" x 2¾"
8	2	1½" x 1¾"
9	2	1" x 2¾"

From selected fabric for the area below the house, cut:

Piece No.	No. of Pieces to Cut	Dimensions
10	1	1½" x 6½"*
11	1	2½" x 6½"*

*I joined 2 different florals for the quilt on the cover: a small wildflower print and a large, stylized tulip print. You can make these strips wider or narrower as you please, as long as the combined measurement is 3½" x 6½". If you want to use only one fabric, cut 1 strip, 3½" x 6½".

PIECING THE HOUSE

1. Pin the chimney pieces (piece #2) with right sides together. Stitch around 3 sides, using a ¼"-wide seam allowance; leave one short end open. Clip the corners and trim the seam allowance to ⅛". Turn right side out and press. Set the chimney aside for now.

2. Sew a roof triangle (piece #1a) and a background triangle (piece #1b) together to make a half-square triangle unit. Press the seam toward the roof triangle. Join the 2 units to make the roof. Press the center seam open.

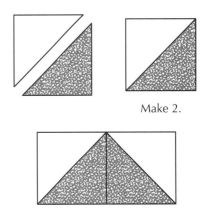

Make 2.

3. Assemble the rest of the house, following the diagram.

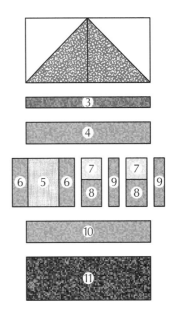

4. Determine where you want to put your chimney. Undo a 1"-wide section of the roof at the desired location. Slip the base of the chimney into the slit, pin, and restitch the seam. You can hand stitch the edges of the chimney in place, or just leave them loose. The weight of the fabric should keep it in place.

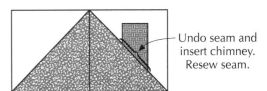

Undo seam and insert chimney. Resew seam.

EMBELLISHMENT IDEAS

➤ Make the chimney out of a "brick" fabric.

➤ Add smoke coming out of the chimney by embroidering a swirling black line or stitching netting or chiffon scraps to look like smoke.

➤ Add a doorknob. Use the same kind of button or bead as you did for the Lighthouse door (see page 38).

➤ Put lace curtains on the windows. They add a nice touch and are easy to attach using fabric glue or a few stitches and scraps of lace.

➤ Stitch, glue, or fuse a flowerpot, kitty, or dachshund in the windows.

➤ Add a path leading from the doorway.

➤ Add flowers under the windows.

➤ Stitch your own house number above the door.

MAKING THE SIDE BORDERS

AT THIS POINT, your Mariner's Compass is surrounded by a Flying Geese border, an accent border, and a plain border. The Picket Fence border has been attached to the bottom, and the Twinkle Star border has been sewn to the top.

Also by now you have completed the Sawtooth Stars, various tree blocks, the Lighthouse and Coast Guard House blocks and are ready to assemble the left and right borders. To make borders like the quilt on the cover, join the blocks in the following order, from top to bottom. Press the seam allowances toward the block with the fewest seams.

Left Border	Right Border
Sawtooth Star	Sawtooth Star
Lodgepole Pine Trees (1 small, 1 large)	Evergreen Tree
Evergreen Tree	Douglas Fir
Filbert Tree	Evergreen Tree
Lodgepole Pine Trees (2 small)	Filbert Tree
Evergreen Tree	Lodgepole Pine Trees (1 small, 1 large)
Lighthouse	Coast Guard House

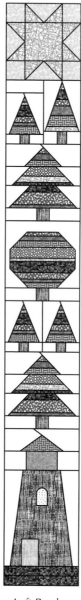

Left Border

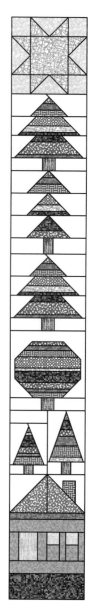

Right Border

Measure the borders to see if they fit the quilt top. If they are too long, don't panic. Simply take up a few seam allowances. The Filbert trees are particularly easy to adjust because they have some space to play with. Start by a taking a little deeper seam allowance. Measure again, and stitch again if necessary.

NOTE: *Taking a deeper seam allowance will also make the trunk on the adjoining tree shorter.*

If this does not seem like it will be enough, take a deeper seam allowance at the bottom of the Lighthouse or Coast Guard House blocks. Do this in the strips below the block, not in the block itself. Measure the borders again. If they fit, stitch them to the sides of the quilt top. Press the seams toward the center of the quilt.

If, on the other hand, one or both of these borders are too short, you will need to add a filler strip. First, determine the amount of background fabric to be added. At this point, it would be more prudent to add a bit too much than too little. Don't forget to add seam allowances, then cut a piece the desired width and 6½" long. Insert the filler strip between two trees. Then measure the border again. If it's just right, sew it to the quilt top. If not, keep adjusting until it fits.

THREE SIMPLE STRIPS

Finished sizes:
1" wide for first strip
1½" wide for second strip
1¼" wide for third strip

THE FIRST STRIP goes above the Twinkle Star border. The second and third strips run along the bottom of the quilt below the Picket Fence border. The choices for these simple strips will vary with your own special quilt. For my quilt on the cover, I chose a celestial fabric for the first strip to continue the theme of the stars. For the bottom, I chose a wheat print and a small-scale pebble print. The wheat resembles the grasses you often see at the beach. The pebbles are just that. I also inserted a section with dachshunds strolling along the beach. This is optional of course, though I think it's wonderful.

CUTTING

From the fabric for the first simple strip, cut:

- 2 strips, each 1½" x 42"

From the fabric for the second simple strip, cut:

- 2 strips, each 2" x 42"

Optional:

- Cut a 2" x 5½" insert strip from a novelty print.

From the fabric for the third simple strip, cut:

- 2 strips, each 1¾" x 42"

ADDING THE STRIPS

1. Join the short ends of the first border strips. Press the seam to one side. Fold the quilt in half vertically and mark the top and bottom center points with a pin. Align the center seam of the first border with the center-point pin at the top of the quilt. Pin the strip in place and stitch. Press the seam toward the strip just added.

2. Join the short ends of the second border strips. Press the seam to one side. Insert the optional novelty print. Choose the placement for the insert. Cut the strip at the point you want the novelty fabric to begin. Insert the novelty print between the two sections. Press the seams to one side.

3. Join the short ends of the third border strips. Press the seam to one side.

4. Pin the second and third border strips together at the center seam. Join the two strips on the long edges. Press the seam toward the third border strip.

5. Align the center seam of the strips with the center-point pin at the bottom of the quilt. Pin the strip in place and stitch. Press the seam toward the second border strip.

SECOND ACCENT BORDER

Finished size: 1" wide

BARGELLO BORDER

Finished size: 7" x 49"

THIS ACCENT BORDER can be the same fabric as the first accent border that surrounds the Flying Geese border. Though narrow, this is also a significant border.

CUTTING

From the fabric for the border, cut:
- 8 strips, 1½" x 42"

ADDING THE BORDER

1. Join the short ends of the strips to make 4 pairs of strips. Press the seams to one side.

2. Referring to the directions for adding borders on page 16, measure, trim, and sew the accent border to the top and bottom edges of the quilt first, then to the sides. Press the seams toward the accent border.

THE BARGELLO PATTERN is a traditional needlepoint design that has been adapted to quilting. The actual methods of piecing vary widely. This particular method is very simple compared to the overall impact achieved.

The key to a successful Bargello border is value. Individual colors of the fabrics are not as important to the overall effect of the Bargello as the changing interplay of the light and dark values of the fabrics. That is not to say the colors you select are not important; choosing fabric from very light to very dark is essential for your Bargello border.

My quilt shown on the cover includes a Bargello border at the top and bottom. This added 14" to the overall length of the quilt and made it into a rectangle. Some students have put a Bargello border all the way around the quilt, keeping it square. This is a great way to increase the quilt to bed size. Consider what size you want your quilt when deciding where to put the Bargello border.

If you decide to place the Bargello border along the sides, as well as the top and bottom, there are two concerns. First, you will need additional 1½"-wide strips of fabric, more than twice the amount specified in the directions. Triple the original yardage to make sure you have enough. The second is, what should you do when the Bargello border intersects at the corners? One solution: don't let it go around the corner. End the border at the edges of the quilt top, and use a 7" x 7" finished square in each corner. Other creative options include making four 7" finished star blocks or four 7" finished Mariner's Compass blocks for the corners. I'm sure you can come up with many more design options.

Another approach to this design problem is to design the Bargello border to intersect at the corners. You could have all the color runs going in the same direction, and whatever happens at the corners, happens! Or, you could change the diagonal orientation of each border. Sketch your ideas on graph paper to see what you can come up with.

The following directions are for two Bargello borders. Each border is made up of seven rows, using twelve different fabrics. The colors will slant diagonally to the left.

CUTTING

From each of the 12 fabrics, cut:
• 5 strips, each 1½" x 21". Keep the fabric strips sorted in individual stacks.

PIECING THE BORDER

1. Arrange the strips in the desired color sequence (fabrics 1–12). Make a total of 5 identical strip units. Press the seams down in 3 of the strip units, and up in the remaining 2. Cut a total of 32 segments, each 1½" wide, from the strip units pressed down. Cut a total of 24 segments, each 1½" wide, from the strip units pressed up. (You will need more segments and, therefore, more strip units if you are making additional borders.) Keep the segments separated in 2 stacks by the direction in which the seams were pressed: one stack pressed down and one stack pressed up.

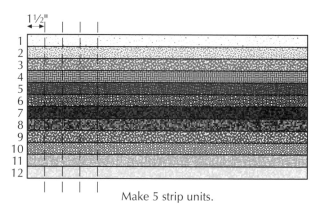

Make 5 strip units.

TIP: *Make sure your vertical cuts are accurate. Use the horizontal seams in the strip unit to help keep your ruler lined up. You may need to square up the cutting edge often.*

2. Join 4 segments end to end to make each of the 14 rows needed for the border. Join the segments pressed in the same direction for each row. Keep the rows in 2 stacks, according to the direction in which the seams were pressed. This will help you sew the rows together later.

Stitch.   Stitch.   Stitch.

3. Starting with a row from the strip units pressed down, and alternating with rows from the strip units pressed up, arrange 7 rows as shown below (top). The row closest to you will be Row 1, the next is Row 2, on up to Row 7 which is the top (and last) row. Offset the rows by one square to the left to create the diagonal movement and the Bargello effect.

4. Following the diagram below (bottom), undo the seams and remove the excess squares from the right end of Rows 1, 2, 3, 4, 5, and 6 and add them to the left end of those rows. You will also be adding an additional square to the extreme left end of each row. There should be a total of 49 squares in each row.

5. Join the rows, pinning the seam intersections to ensure a perfect match. Press the seams in one direction.

6. Repeat steps 3–5 to make the second Bargello border strip.

7. Stitch the Bargello border strips to the top and bottom of your quilt. Press the seams toward the accent border.

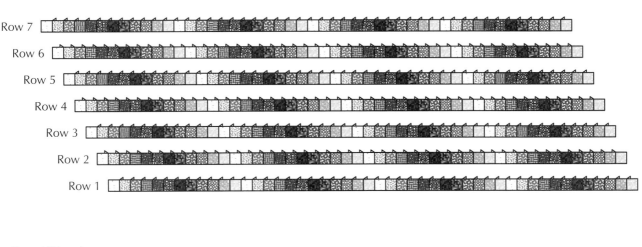

Row 7
Row 6
Row 5
Row 4
Row 3
Row 2
Row 1

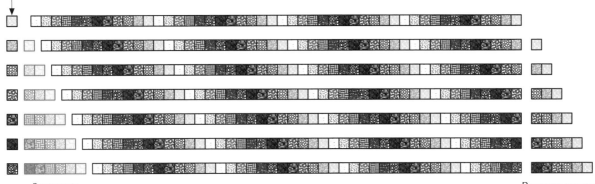

Cut additional
1½" x 1½" squares
and add to front
of each row.

Segments
added
from ends
of rows.

Remove squares
from these rows
and add to front.

LAST TWO BORDERS

Finished size: 7" x 49"

MARINER'S COMPASS CENTER

CUTTING

From the fabric for the narrow border, cut:

- 8 strips, each 1½" x 42"

From the fabric for the outer border, cut:

- 8 strips, each 7½" x 42"

ADDING THE BORDERS

1. Join the short ends of the 1½"-wide strips to make 4 pairs of strips. Press the seams to one side.

2. Referring to the directions for adding borders on page 16, measure, trim, and sew the narrow borders to the quilt. Press the seams away from the center of the quilt.

3. Repeat steps 1 and 2 with the 7½"-wide outer border strips.

Congratulations! You have just stitched the final border to your Mariner's Medallion quilt. Now you're ready to appliqué the center of the Mariner's Compass.

THE CENTER OF the entire quilt—and the quilt's focus—is at the center of the Mariner's Compass. I strongly recommend that you finish the rest of your quilt top before you add the center. You want to allow the quilt to develop its personality! Although you began with a design, color, and theme, this quilt will quickly become an autobiography. Along the way, as you learn new techniques and experiment with different color combinations, you will be blending this knowledge with your previous experiences. Consequently, by waiting, you will choose a more interesting and artistic center.

The center of my quilt, shown on the cover and on page 17, is a chrysanthemum blossom cut from an antique kimono. I chose this for two reasons. First, the colors and circular shapes complement the rest of the quilt. Second, my husband and I have a large flower garden, and this autumn flower is one of our favorites. I auditioned many different fabrics before I finally selected this chrysanthemum as my Mariner's Compass center.

The most obvious strategy for selecting your center is to use a fabric or its coordinate already in your quilt. However, you can get very creative! One of my students included orcas (killer whales); another used silk-ribbon flowers she had embroidered. One student reduced the scale of the outer Mariner's Compass, paper-pieced it the same way, and placed the smaller Mariner's

Compass in the center of the larger one. On "The Compass to Color" (page 18), I embroidered a Mariner's Compass, using the same colors of rayon thread as the larger pieced compass. Embroidery machines offer many possibilities!

All of these centers look as if the designer had planned the entire quilt around the center, when, in fact, it was just the opposite! The process of making the quilt guided them to the perfect choice.

Additional design sources are thrift stores and garage sales. You may already have something stashed at home that you have forgotten about. It could be an old embroidery or needlepoint, a piece of lace or an old silk tie. I believe that all those little things we save actually belong in a project we just haven't made yet! So, think hard, find that perfect center, and sew it in.

Once you've made your selection, I've found the following method the easiest for achieving a perfect circle.

1. Cut out your circle, using the template on page 50. This template includes seam allowances.

TIP: *Use transparent template material for the circle. This way, if you have chosen a center that is directional in any way, you will be able to see and cut it accordingly.*

2. With your ¼" foot or guide, follow the edge and stitch around the circle. Use a moderate stitch length. Leave your thread tails intact. (You may also want to mark the stitching line with a water-erasable pen, and use that as a stitching guide.)

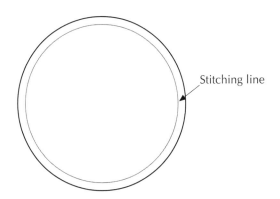

Stitching line

3. Gently pull one of the threads, not so tight as you would a gathered garment, but enough that the outline of the circle pops out and the edges turn under, creating a ¼" seam allowance. Carefully press along this new edge.

4. Find the center of your Mariner's Compass. Fold the center circle (the one you just pressed) in half twice to find its center. Place a pin at each of these points, then position the center circle on the quilt. Begin pinning the circle in place at each of the seam points of Fabric 6 in your compass. Even if this somewhat distorts your circle, I feel it is more important to match the seams than to have a perfect circle. Most people will never notice a slight discrepancy in your circle.

5. Using a blindstitch, hand stitch the center in place. Use a thread that best matches the center, not the background. After you have completed the stitching, remove the machine basting and press the top.

Your center may need more detail work. Decide if it is appropriate to do it now or when you do the quilting.

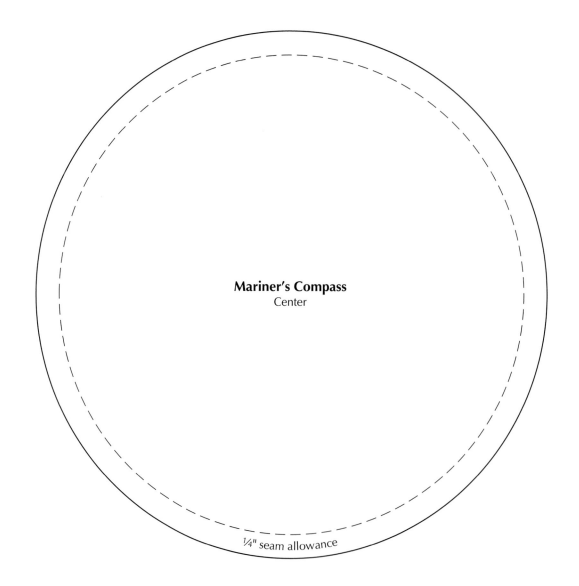

Mariner's Compass
Center

¼" seam allowance

FROM QUILT TOP TO QUILT

BEFORE YOUR QUILT can really be called a quilt, it must be quilted and labeled. In addition, it must be bound and a sleeve pocket added for hanging. Completing projects, for some, is an abstract concept; for others, it is a religion. I fall into the latter category. This in no way infers that a project once begun must be completed in a prescribed amount of time. Nor does it specify that you have only a certain number of projects running concurrently. It simply means that until that project is quilted and bound, it is still a *project*!

I believe there are more reasons *not* to conclude a project than there are to complete one. The emotional energy that accompanies your new undertaking is long gone! The baby you were making a quilt for is grown. Your quilt group or guild has yet another new and exciting challenge. New classes, fabric, books, patterns, and magazines are constantly enticing you. And, ultimately, starting new projects is just more fun! So find out what it takes to motivate you to finish a quilt, and do it. Here are some strategies my students have shared:

➤ Make a date with a quilting friend to sew—and keep it!

➤ Devise incentives for completing a particular project.

➤ Take advantage of quilt shops that offer free classroom time to work on incomplete quilt tops.

➤ Sign up for classes offering assistance in completing your work.

➤ Only purchase more fabric after one of your projects is finished.

➤ Have the project professionally machine quilted.

When I became burdened with too many "works in progress," I began a project journal. All of my quilting projects were listed, whether they were a class sample, a competition piece, a quilt to be published, a charitable donation, a gift for a relative, or something for my own home. My sister pointed out that even if I finished one quilt a month, it would still take years to clear up my list!

To find a workable situation, it was necessary to come up with a strategy for myself. I decided to complete one project a week, or four a month. This was a bold plan. Workable? Yes, because the list created a new challenge. Though a formidable task, these projects had to be done! When I completed a quilt, I put the date in my journal. The satisfaction of finally completing something was so great that it empowered me to continue with the plan. Try a strategy or two that you think will work for you. Good luck!

LABELING YOUR QUILT

FOR HISTORICAL REASONS, a comprehensive label is very important. And, yes, your work is important enough for a label! This is not just for your benefit, but for your family and any other lucky persons who will admire your quilt through the years!

I like to make labels about 4" x 7" so that I can include a lot of information on them. If your sewing machine has a lettering system, use it! You can hand embroider the letters as well, or hand letter your label with a permanent fabric pen. There are also many new photo-transfer techniques that work well.

It may be helpful to use Stitch-n-Tear or interfacing to help stabilize the label while you are lettering on it. Some of my labels are pieced quilt sections I am not using in the quilt. This is fun and a time-saver. It also ties the quilt top to the back.

Your labels should include the following information:

➤ The name of the quilt

➤ Your full name

➤ Your business name, if applicable

➤ Your city, county, province and/or state, and country

➤ The date

➤ Who the quilt was made for, if you made it for a specific person or event

This additional identification is also worth including:

➤ What series it belongs to, if your quilt is part of a series

➤ A teacher's name, if applicable

➤ A story that is connected with the piece, especially a heartfelt one

I know. It seems crazy to think that all of this will fit on one label! So maybe you need two or three labels, in different sizes and different shapes. Add some artwork. Hand embroider a motif that is becoming to the quilt, or a motif that is significant to you. You could start a personal history with your own logo! This logo may also be incorporated into the quilt top. For me, a dachshund usually appears on my labels, as well as somewhere on the quilt top.

If you are fortunate enough to own or have access to an embroidery machine, use it! With little effort, these machines produce amazing labels. I can usually find a disc with a theme similar to the quilt I'm labeling.

Also, I have used patches, decals, buttons, ribbon, and a myriad of other things I have collected over the years. I simply hand or machine stitch them to the larger label.

TIP: *When is the correct time to attach your label? You can sew it to the lower right corner of the quilt back before it is basted or quilted. Or, you can attach your label after the quilting is complete.*

Your label can be as creative and wonderful as you desire! Initially, it will take time to set up a format that you like, but it is well worth the effort. Once you're comfortable with the label format, you can duplicate it for other quilts, adjusting the pertinent information as needed.

CHOOSING THE BATTING

THERE ARE AS many different battings—and opinions about them—as there are quilters! I am an advocate of a moderate-weight cotton batting for wall hangings and most bed quilts. I am not a hand quilter, so the heavier cotton battings work well for me. The newer cotton battings do not require the close quilting that the older ones did. They are also much easier to care for.

If you have a specific reason to use polyester batting, use it. Polyester is nice for children's bed quilts, or if you prefer a loftier look.

PREPARING FOR QUILTING

1. Cut your backing and batting about 4" larger than the quilt top.

2. Lay the backing, right side down, on a clean, flat surface; secure with masking tape. (The fabric needs to be taut, but not stretched.)

Lay the batting on top of the backing and secure with tape. Add the quilt top, right side up; secure with tape.

3. Beginning in the center, hand baste every 4" horizontally, then vertically. I prefer hand basting over other methods because I can then machine quilt without stopping to remove pins.

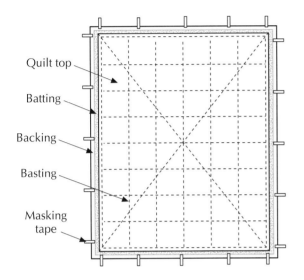

Quilt top

Batting

Backing

Basting

Masking tape

4. After basting, remove the tape. You are ready to quilt!

QUILTING YOUR QUILT

YOUR MARINER'S MEDALLION may be quilted in many different ways. A combination of techniques looks great. For the quilt shown on the cover, I chose to machine stipple, outline stitch, and stitch in-the-ditch. The stippling was done with cotton threads in gold and yellows to coordinate with the many background fabrics. The outline stitching was done in cotton threads that matched the fabrics they were stitched on. Much of the in-the-ditch work was done in gold metallic thread—a subtle, but nice touch.

Hand quilting is always appropriate. Though time-consuming, it is well worth the effort. Tying the quilt with decorative threads is another option. Furthermore, a professional machine quilter usually has many suggestions and patterns, and can often combine overall patterns with meandering and stippling. You are the best judge of the quilting methods that will complement your work.

I enjoy designing machine-quilting patterns as I go, working on the spur of the moment. I may start with a vague overall plan, though doing my own work allows me to "just do it" as I go! Some very good machine quilting books are on the market, but my favorite is *Machine Quilting Made Easy* by Maurine Noble. It is also a good idea to take a class and practice.

SQUARING UP YOUR QUILT

WHEN YOU HAVE completed the quilting, it is time to square up your quilt; this means cutting off the excess backing and batting, as well as cleaning up any threads or uneven sections of border. Using the seam from the last border as a guide, place the ruler on this line, then measure out to the edge of the quilt in a number of places. Take your narrowest measurement, then use it to position your ruler and cut off the excess.

Next, fold the quilt, then fold it again in the other direction. Does your quilt have nice square corners and edges that correspond with each other? If not, this is your last chance to correct it. Use a large square ruler to square up the corners.

Use a basting or serpentine stitch around the edge to stabilize the quilt. *Do not use a zigzag stitch.* Now you are ready for the final process: binding.

BINDING YOUR QUILT

TRADITIONALLY, THE BINDING color is the darkest color in the quilt, or it is the same fabric as that used in the final border. Now that you know this rule, you have permission to do whatever you want! I like to continue the theme of the final border in the binding. For instance, if your final border is a floral, I would use more flowers for the binding fabric.

The construction of your binding is very important; it is the last finishing detail of your quilt. My work as a judge in quilt competitions has made this very clear to me. Participants often overlook the importance of the binding. The following binding method combines the best in detail, strength, and beauty.

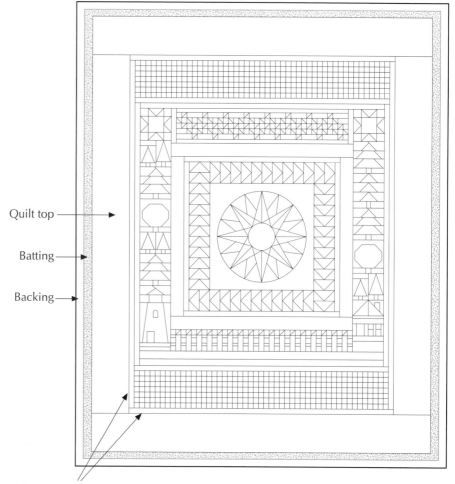

Quilt top

Batting

Backing

Use these seam lines as a guide
for squaring up the quilt.

1. Calculate the amount of binding you need by adding the measurements from each side, plus 10" for the corners. Cut your binding fabric into 3"-wide crosswise strips (across the width of the fabric). I cut on the bias only if I want to take advantage of a plaid print, or use rounded corners on my quilt.

2. Join strips at right angles and stitch across the corner as shown. Trim excess fabric; press the seams open.

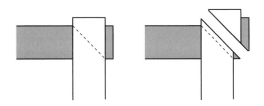

3. Fold the binding in half lengthwise, wrong sides together, and press.

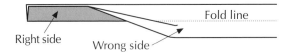

To attach your binding, start in the upper left-hand corner of your quilt, about 10" from the corner. Leave a 4" tail of binding fabric.

1. Lay the binding on top of the quilt, raw edges together. Begin stitching, using a ½"-wide seam allowance.

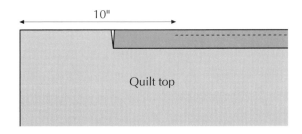

2. Stitch about 2", stop, and cut the threads. Remove the quilt from the machine and fold the binding to the back; it should barely

cover the stitching line you just made. If the binding overlaps too much, stitch again just *inside* the first stitching line. Not enough to cover the original stitching? Stitch just *outside* the original stitching. Take out the excess stitches before you proceed.

3. When you have determined the correct placement of the seam, stitch to within ½" of the first corner. Stop, cut the thread, and remove the quilt from the machine.

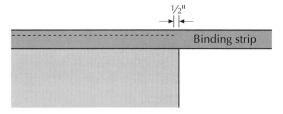

4. Fold the binding to create a mitered corner. Now continue stitching to the next corner. Repeat the mitering process at each corner.

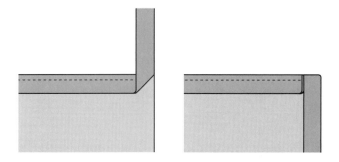

5. After turning the last corner, stitch about 3" and stop. Make sure you have at least a 4" overlap of the two ends of the binding. Cut the threads and remove the quilt from the machine. Measure a 3" overlap and trim off the extra binding.

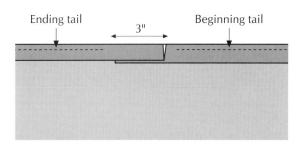

6. Lay out the quilt top, right side up. Place the unfolded, unstitched tails, right sides together, at right angles and pin. Draw a line from the upper left-hand corner to the lower right-hand corner of the binding. Stitch along this line.

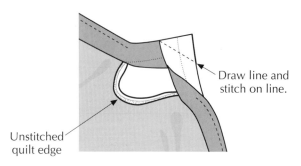

Draw line and stitch on line.

Unstitched quilt edge

7. Carefully trim the seam allowances to ¼" and press the seam open. Refold the binding in half again and press. Finish stitching the binding to the quilt.

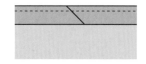

8. Turn the binding to the back of the quilt; pin in place. I pin approximately 12" at a time. Hand stitch the binding to the quilt back, matching the thread to the binding and carefully mitering the corners as you approach them. Hand stitch down each side of the mitered corners. Continue in this fashion until you have completely sewn the binding to the quilt.

ADDING A SLEEVE POCKET

A SLEEVE POCKET is very important for displaying your quilt on a wall. This is the last step in my quilting process.

1. Cut a 7½"-wide strip of backing fabric; if the quilt is wider than 40", you will need to cut 2 strips and stitch them together, end to end. Cut the strip 1" shorter than the width of your quilt. Fold the short ends under ¼", stitch, and press.

2. Fold the pocket the long way, right sides together; stitch and press. Turn the pocket right side out and press again.

3. Find the center point of the top edge of the quilt, as well as the center point of the sleeve pocket. Pin the pocket and quilt together, with the folded edge of the pocket next to the binding. Blindstitch this edge.

Baste sleeve to top next to binding.

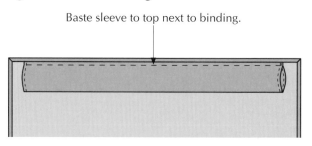

4. Push the bottom edge of the sleeve up just a bit. This provides a little give so the hanging rod doesn't put strain on the quilt. Blindstitch the bottom of the sleeve. Take care not to catch the front of the quilt as you stitch.

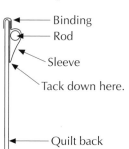

Binding
Rod
Sleeve
Tack down here.

Quilt back